From the "publisher"

Tyler tweeted to the world that he was looking for a publisher. I replied. Within the shortest time possible, we had the first version of *Newspaper Drumsticks* on Amazon. This was during the early days of Covid. The reviews were many, thoughtful and positive. Tyler's years of work gave us a playful—yet sobering—look at what it truly means to be in "lockdown".

Now, as masks are no longer required, we are launching a proper version of *Newspaper Drumsticks*; one that is less of a fragile signal flare, and more of a well-made torch. *Newspaper Drumsticks* is a classic, as profoundly simple (and American) as *Blades of Grass*. Tyler has transformed his brother's observations about life in a constant vicious circle of bureaucracy into Zen-like poems, as meaningful and brief as ripples in a pond.

Stephen Black
Toledo, Ohio
May 26, 2021

Newspaper Drumsticks

Tyler Dempsey

Poems sent to a brother in Alaska from a prison in Oklahoma

Copyright © 2021 Tyler Dempsey

All rights reserved. No part of this publication may be produced, distributed, or transmitted in any forms by any means, including photocopying, recording, or other electronic or mechanical methods, without the prior written consent of the publisher, except in the case of brief quotations embodied in critical reviews and certain other non-commercial uses permitted by copyright law. For permission requests, please contact the publisher.

978-0-578-25373-2 (Ebook)
978-0-578-25374-9 (Paperback)

Book Merah

Content

Preface	1
New Environment	5
A Portion of Joy in the Puzzle of Life	7
Encounter with a Guard	9
Hindrances	11
I Must Become Nothing	13
I Won't Be Inert	15
Letters	17
I have a New Job	19
I'm Tired of People	21
Been Reading	23
DOC has Moved Over-40	25
Prison got me this Reverse Engineering Degree	27
Took a Broken Hot Pot	29
I can Read Music!	31
I Hate these Situations	33
150 Mph Winds	35
Associating with others of Like Mind	37
Feet of those who Bring Good News	39

Friend is a Second Self	41
Ginosko	43
Protein	45
I'm Glad you told me what you did	47
Interdependence of Opposites	49
Been in a Rut	51
I've Picked up the Drums Again	53
Money	55
People in Here	57
Reader Interpretation	59
Prison is having a Shakedown	61
Delicacies of Prison	63
The Kosher Diet is probably the Best	65
The Soil of our Lives	67
Thinking of Papa and Nana	69
The Tallest Mountain in my Life	71
They Opened the Yard	73
Vanity all within our Passions	75
Travis Dempsey #611192	77
Acknowledgements	79
Author Bio	81

Preface

As I write, in April of 2020, COVID-19 continues to make fresh graves worldwide. In yachts, in shacks, in villas, in houses, and in all kinds of rooms, people avoid the plague. Those who gamble on going outside are mindful of social distancing.

In America, 2.3 million prisoners cannot go outside, nor social distance. My brother: I cry when I read his letters, cry because of what is happening to him, cry because of his beautiful, unwanted wisdom. Cry because he is alone, 4000 miles away.

Friends, lovers, spouses, and parents. Children. Prisoners need these people in their lives, yet fear that pain and grief and shame will forever flicker through these relationships.

……………..

"Prison" is many things: a dictator, an education system, a lover. Control is exclusion. Whatever the guise, control results in shame—a long-term disease.

Prisons. Halls of Congress. Societal "Norms." The mechanisms of control are only visible to those who profit from them or those who suffer by them. We who are outside of prisons are very distant from them. This book's hope is to decrease that distance.

I'm a curator of my brother's words. His words have given me grace, humility, and humor. I want to share them, share them so far that they return to their source. I pray that this book isn't a time capsule, but something that grows to transcend shame.

It's Spring, and the anemones are blooming. "Daughters of the wind." Flying like butterflies. May they fly to you.

We're alone, together.
T.D
April, 2020

Newspaper Drumsticks

New Environment

Like Alaska,
  it too
    has dangerous
      wild
animals
  lurking   about.

I think   I
    would rather face a grizzly!

But
    also   it has beauties,
not on scale.

I am at Mack Alford
Prison
      in Stringtown.

I will be here a while.

We have a
    church,   Christian
library,
regular   library,
gym,   track,   workout area,

softball
  field,
      college
and school area, and a
manufacturing center.

Compared to
   Okmulgee,
it's "Alaskish:"

broad, big, beautiful.

A Portion of Joy in the Puzzle of Life

Oh
   goodness!

It was   awesome
   cool water

to a parched
   soul

            hearing from
                you.

You've captivated
   prayers.

   Not worry—

longing,

solid communication

   only we have.

Encounter with a Guard

Exiting our building
······················· heading for the cafeteria,
I spoke a simple greeting,
met with discourtesy.

I thought nothing of it.

Hindrances

merely   seeds
of opportunity.

I Must Become Nothing

My daily
  goal
      to decrease

more   and more.

      Speak my mind

to the one
person   I was honest
with
      growing up.

Our lives
     the spokes of a wheel,

  connected,
    yet altogether independent
   even still connected.

If
   I could have seen this
when I was
  out.

I Won't Be Inert

I see a lot
in
  myself
      that
need
  be
      pruned.

Hard

    waiting

for
           scissors.

Letters

Mean everything.

Please,
write soon.

I have a New Job

It's telemarketing.
        The ass   that calls
during dinner.

Pays $1.45 an hour.
        Cream-of-the-crop.

I'm Tired of People

Our cell
became   hang-out
for good guys
         and Christians.

It's great,   I
   just
need alone   time
it's wearing me out.

My mind
racing
   for ways
   to retreat
a   home
      to renew strength.

Been Reading

Star Wars
    books.

All   I can find.

  Watched the movies
now
  I'm
              trying

     to find   the books.

Choices
are
ok.

There are   two
   or
three book
series
  we have
one   of.

If you   find

Star Wars

books

anywhere
send them in.

DOC has Moved Over-40

inmates
to a   facility
  going over-40
only

and   moved younger knuckleheads into

  the vacancy.

Things are tense.

Don't know if it's
  the heat
  of summer
or what,

the crash dummies
    are in full force.

Tension   high as the temperature.

Prison got me this Reverse Engineering Degree

Take Oreo cookies

separate them
add milk cook in the microwave to make cake.

Add peanut butter candy
bars
for icing.

2 sleeves Ritz
half bag Cheetos.
Crunch add milk until dough.

Form into pizza

shape

microwave until almost done.

Top with saucemeat veggiescheese finish microwaving have the best Not-Pizza you'll ever have.
I'm fat.

Took a Broken Hot Pot

and   made
 a
      grill.

Had it
   a month
 or so

      it changes
                  everything.

Grilled cheese
          grilled
burritos

for the Super Bowl

make a quesadilla.

  Delicious
whole   pod   smells
bomb.

I can Read Music!

Know terms:
    flam, paradiddle.

The Rosetta Stone of Drumming.

I
  practice
in the cell,

then   incorporate
at
  church.

Not sure if that's kosher.

  But that's what I do.

I'm all about sound
and   experimenting
  with the
              tool.
Intro'd
   a song
       with a
straight tom-opener.

Flowed off the tom.
 8th beat, adding beats on the up-and tom-tom'ing the hell out of it.

I Hate these Situations

I cannot
  comfort

  and weep
    with everyone

Miles away
         hurt

  alone

      why?

May we not lose   heart
  our hope.

150 Mph Winds

allow for construction

       something
  new.

Winds   are
  good:

the weak strengthens,
dead becomes
new,
    garbage blows   away.

Associating with others of Like Mind

I have a few
   here

  can   count
them
  on one hand.

Even
   here
friends.

Feet of those who Bring Good News

Communication
  with
    those I love.

Delightful

    comfort

in
dark.

Thank you so much for being there.

  It has been
hot   and
  sweaty
but it is summer.

Friend is a Second Self

To see, you

again   soon,

   through
 your
 eyes.

Plant
    mine
on nature, unaltered by concrete
    steel.

The sky:
painting
            genuine,
      I enjoy that all   the more.

Ginosko

Wisdom
  a small irritant.

One   writes
a book
    on how to handle trials

but until you experience it.

A flower
bruised   underfoot
rewards with perfume.

Love is the skin of knowing.

I'm Glad you told me what you did

though you
   scold
yourself for doing.

I feel that way.

Every
    woman
I
    felt it

every job

I
said,
"I don't understand!"

If you figure
   it out,
do tell.

Protein

I'm still
between pay on jobs,
unable to buy protein

so now they tell me what   to eat.

Was   getting
          150
grams

of protein,

now
I'm lucky to

get
  50.

Once   I get
caught
          up   on
                    things
               I hope I can afford a little   more
protein.

Interdependence of Opposites

  Just read
a book
    on evil.

Good   and   evil,

pain
troubles, triumphs.

Our relationship
  reached
levels   it
never   could

given circumstances
    at present.

Pity I was too proud.

Foolish
    with life and family.

Forgive me.

Living   and enjoying,
enslaved,   ever free,
under authority
mastering
   all.

Been in a Rut

Try to   laugh
         stay
positive.

     Contagious
        place.

 Same scenery
     food,
clothes

        day
over and over. Poor Bill   Murray.

I'm alone.
   I feel alone.

Prison: interdiction from loved ones.

Seen   for what
     they
   are
it controls you.

No changing that.
I'm alone.

Zero
  solution
         finished.
Forlorn
         drawn to a love story to
  p   l a c a t e.

  I'm a loser.

Your life thrusts   forward,

  mine
   increasingly
  torpid.

I've Picked up the Drums Again

Am preparing.
I made some
 drum sticks out of newspapers.

Money

Please,
send money.

If you can
birthday money
  early

I've gotten myself in
  a bind
    with some   guys

send money.

  Could use cash

if you
    or mom
          could bless the books

I need   socks
  shoes
toothpaste
stamps
underwear
  shaving cream

couple
hundred bucks.
Anything.

I know times are hard   for you.

Please, send money.

People in Here

wake   up defeated.

It's
  in their heart
as I look them in the eye.

Hear it   behind
speech
coated in sweetness.

I thought
how I would be in the future.

Will I
     slip   into the canyon
  of discontent,

                    a river of self-pity?

Reader Interpretation

is
  so
    often
different
from Author Interpretation.

Good vocabulary
  and
communication   narrow
     the distance
  between the two.

I'm not good at that.

Prison is having a Shakedown

At work
  but will go   back
to
an earthquake.

Still making calls.

Inmate,
        calling   the
White House,
        Pentagon,
   F B I,
Langley,   Congress,
military bases,   government agencies.

I feel important

or that I'm not an

  inmate.

Voice
        hides gray
   and fence:
Just words
 ideas.

Delicacies of Prison

Ramen,
    beans, sardines,
and hot sauce,

mixed in harmony.

The Kosher Diet is probably the Best

They get cereal
fruit for breakfast,

and a small, nutritious T.V. dinner.

The Soil of our Lives

Every word,
  action,

        happenstance.

Faith
is lava

    ever-making
acres
              and acres
of new land.

Destroying me
my geography,
creating
    a man.

Thinking of Papa and Nana

   Prompted

by
people
  who   recently
  lost

grandparents

or in the

   process.

One single
point
   they exist.

Memories, seclusion.

  Make them,

and enjoy people

the only ones
             of value.

The Tallest Mountain in my Life

For the first time
    I can see

what I easily   neglected.

Aspects
   in my life
took for granted,

 now   the things I really long for.

All that
   me
   slip through my hands
slide out.

When I
ascend the   peak,
I will hold a better view

of   eternity.

They Opened the Yard

We
   sort of
have free   roam.

Bad thing
     is
I've been working   so much
    I can't get out.

Putting
in   12-hour days

6-days-a-week.

Vanity all within our Passions

Good or
 great.
  Remember   the

old
 quote,

"Jack of all trades . . ."

 Dump
resources
into
 so   much
 life.

We're exhausted

 nothing

to show.

 What the hell are we doing?

Travis Dempsey #611192

Mack Alford Correctional Center

BS-131

PO Box 220

Stringtown, OK 74569

(The above address is no longer valid.)

Acknowledgements

Enormous gratitude to my brother, without whom these wouldn't exist. I am forever indebted to Stephen Black, and Book Merah, for making this a reality. Also to the journals where some of these poems found a first home: "Ginosko," "Associating with others of Like Mind," Malarkey Books; "Friend is a Second Self," "Feet of those who Bring Good News," "I must become Nothing," Mineral Lit Mag; "Prison got me this Reverse-Engineering Degree," Emerge Literary Journal; "Protein," "150 Mph Winds," Re-side Zine.

Author Bio

Tyler Dempsey won the second annual The Tulsa Voice/Nimrod International Journal Flash Fiction Competition. His stories, poems, and essays appear in journals online and in print. Find him on Twitter @tylercdempsey, or online at http://tylerdempseywriting.com. He lives and works in Alaska.

Travis Dempsey was arrested in February 2009.

Stephen Black and Tyler Dempsey would like to thank Joseph Rushmore for his photographic work for the covers.

josephrushmore.com
josephrushmore@gmail.com

Book Merah

Book Merah, started by Stephen Black in 2007, publishes books, ebooks, traditional art and media projects, as well as content for AR and VR.

Titles

The following titles are available on Amazon and through Ingram Spark, except *Contact With Shadow*, which is at https://unglue.it/work/137647/

Fires by Cyril Wong.

Cyril is an internationally recognized poet from Singapore.

The following books are by Stephen Black, who is a writer, visual artist and producer of events, TV, AR and music. He is also the founder and curator of Maith, the world's first exhibition space dedicated to AR exhibitions. www.blacksteps.tv

Obama Search Words

Dynamic, fact-based fiction about Obama's life until just before he became President. Includes charts and color photos.

Furikake

If you like Japanese rice seasonings, glimpses of Singaporean life and canoeing in the Happy Isles of Oceania, this is the book for you.

Contact With Shadow

Life-shattering heartbreak, molecular cooking and the history of pre-Linotype printing in Singapore. Part PhD thesis, part stream of consciousness.

i ate tiong bahru (second edition)

iatb's short stories combine food, history, architecture and personal memoir to celebrate the community spirit that once defined Tiong Bahru. A bestseller in Singapore.

Bali Wave Ghost

A reality TV star returns to Bali twenty years after the explosive event which changed his life.

Red Dot SAAD

Glimpses into one man's artistic life in Singapore and Bali. A journal made of orchids, polygons and banana leaves.

Bubiko Foodtour's Unusual Guide to Augmented Reality

For three years, Stephen Black and Sayuri Okayama researched AR and the food of Southeast Asia. Bubiko Foodtour soon tagged along. Based on lessons learned from that time as well as a subsequent world-wide tour.

Look for Bubiko on Instagram and other social media.

Instagram
instagram.com/bubikofoodtour/

twitter
@bookmerah

Facebook
facebook.com/BookMerah

Book Merah is now finalizing discussions with poet **Jennifer Anne Champion**, whose works include *Caterwaul*, published by Math Paper Press; and *A History of Clocks*, published by Redwheelbarrow Books.

https://jenniferannechampion.com

www.ingramcontent.com/pod-product-compliance
Lightning Source LLC
Chambersburg PA
CBHW072016290426
44109CB00018B/2260